CW00956458

EXEUNT - THE STAGE DOOR PROJECT

EXEUNT

THE STAGE DOOR PROJECT

LLOYD MCDONAGH • SALVATORE SCARPA

RENARD PRESS LTD

Kemp House
152–160 City Road
London EC1V 2NX
United Kingdom
info@renardpress.com
020 8050 2928

www.renardpress.com

Exeunt: The Stage Door Project first published by Renard Press Ltd in 2021

Design and images © Lloyd McDonagh and Salvatore Scarpa
Text © the authors, 2021

Thanks are given to the authors for permission to publish their words.

Design by Lloyd McDonagh and Salvatore Scarpa

Printed in Istanbul by AllNote Printing
www.allnote.co.uk

Hardback ISBN: 978-1-913724-75-7

9 8 7 6 5 4 3 2 1

This book is dedicated to the theatre industry.

Proceeds from this book will go to charities that support theatres and the professionals who work to keep them alive.

With contributions by

Dame Judi Dench ● Emma Rice ● Ned Seago ● Simon Callow ● John McCrea
Diane Page ● Reece Shearsmith ● Anita Dobson ● Macy Nyman ● David Bedella
Kwong Loke ● Luke Giles ● Stephanie Street ● Dame Harriet Walter
Rebecca Frecknall ● David Jonsson ● Jackie Clune ● Ben Cracknell
Richard Sutton ● Adeyinka Akinrinade ● Le Gateau Chocolat ● Paule Constable
Lucian Msamati ● Adrian Scarborough ● David Acton ● Natalie Law
Gordon Millar ● Leanne Robinson ● Thomas Aldridge ● Katrina Lindsay
Eben Figueiredo ● Andy Taylor ● Aimie Atkinson ● Jack Holden ● Laura Donnelly
Laurie Kynaston ● Abraham Popoola ● Oengus MacNamara ● Louis Maskell
Valda Aviks ● Garry Cooper ● Mark Dugdale ● Lyn Paul ● James Graham
Emma Sheppard ● Paul Bazely ● Preston Nyman ● Lauren Ward
Jessica Hung Han Yun ● Natalie McQueen ● Gavin Spokes ● Niamh Cusack
Paterson Joseph ● Anna Fleischle ● Daniel Monks ● Michael Sheen ● Lia Williams
Ruthie Henshall ● Simon Lipkin ● Tom Brooke ● Ian Rickson ● Rufus Hound
Zoë Tapper ● Patsy Ferran ● Joshua McGuire ● Sharon D Clarke ● Mark Gatiss
Taz Skylar ● Marianne Benedict ● Ferdinand Kingsley ● Lez Brotherston
Tamsin Withers ● Hadley Fraser ● Karl Queensborough ● Neil Salvage
Jessie Hart ● Kathy Peacock ● Howard Hudson ● Jonathan Andrew Hume
Andy Nyman ● Andrew McDonald ● Claire Roberts ● Michael Jibson
Jason Pennycooke ● Christopher Tendai ● Laura Baldwin ● Matt Henry
Robert Lindsay ● Simon Evans ● Fisayo Akinade ● Irvine Iqbal ● Zoë Wanamaker

CONTENTS

EXEUNT - THE STAGE DOOR PROJECT

INTRODUCTION

All the world's a stage,
And all the men and women merely players;
They have their exits and their entrances...
and their stage doors.

In 2020, for the first time in centuries, there were no theatres open in London.

As two actors who felt that they had lost their homes away from home, we turned to another form of art that could survive the pandemic - photography. *Exeunt - The Stage Door Project* is a collection of memories - images by us and words by theatre luminaries you know and love - brought together to document the effects of the coronavirus pandemic on London's West End.

Who in this industry doesn't dream of walking through the theatrical pearly gates, of feeling the chaos of London's streets being replaced by the ethereal calm of backstage preparations, of gently being reminded to sign in (and out) by the angels at the door?

This book is a tribute to the magical experience that occurs at the stage door. But most of all, it's a celebration of the legendary places, the industry professionals and the countless audience members who weathered the storm together.

Ours is a book to celebrate what we endured together.

All of us.

Lloyd McDonagh & Salvatore Scarpa

Ernie Davis was stage doorman at The Old Vic when I was there in 1960 when we did *She Stoops to Conquer* with Tommy Steele. Tommy received a letter from a fan asking him to sing 'Little White Bull' during the show that night as he was attending with an elderly relation!! Ernie loved the letter so much he asked Tommy if he could keep it… and he did. Stage doormen are rare and marvellous people.

Dame Judi Dench

As a Director, it is not often that I enter through a stage door. There is usually a lonely route to the auditorium through front of house which delivers me straight to my makeshift desk. Directors tend to slip into a theatre alone as actors throng and giggle their way to dressing rooms filled with cards and keepsakes, charms and sweet smells. So, when I think of stage doors, I think of times when I am off duty, anonymous and relaxingly not in charge; a stage door Johnnie if you like! My partner works in the theatre and it is a great joy for me to go and meet him from work; usually at The Old Vic in London. I love to loiter opposite the stage door in the knowledge that he will soon appear. It is at these times, stood in the road, basking in the warmth of the neon that I remember the fairy dust that theatre sprinkles onto our lives. The excitement of not knowing who will pop out of that magic door is intoxicating; it could be a wardrobe assistant, a star or the love of my life. The stage door is a gateway to such electric endeavour, a world of colour, surprise, possibility and potential. This door is the gateway to all I love and all I believe in – and I tingle with a humble sense of gratitude that I am lucky enough to be part of it. Then Simon appears in a chaos of bags and banter with the stage door keeper – and all my dreams come true at once. I get to whisk him to a warm bar for a debrief, decompress and a slow digestion of the day's events. The memory of these nights, this peek into the ephemeral wonder of the telling of stories, has a sweet neon glow and a melancholic sense of loss. When we come back, will the magnificent, messy, mysterious chaos of humanity return? I hope with my whole tired heart that it will.

Emma Rice

In the late 80s, the old stage door outside light was nicked. I rounded the corner of Webber Street and noticed the globe had gone, and when the LX department arrived to work I asked if they were working on it. No they were not, in fact they hadn't seen it was gone. Whoever made away with it had sawn through the swan-neck bracket and wiring. We never discovered who or why.

One morning in 1988 I arrived for work to find the whole of the stage door interior and staircases awash. At that time the stairs were carpeted and the aroma of damp, old, and not necessarily pristine carpet is certainly not to be sniffed at. It stank! Somebody, again we never found out who, had broken the above dressing room window and delivered an incendiary device. The sprinkler system had done its work and damage. Structurally this was insignificant, but we've never had carpeted stairways since.

In 2001, a show called *Over the Moon* was rehearsing with us before doing a short tour and then returning to our stage. On one particular afternoon there was no rehearsing done. Around the old radio I then had (before we hit the 20th century at the Vic with a stage door computer) were gathered Joan Collins, Ray Cooney (director), Moira Lister and Frank Langella, all listening to news from New York. The date was September 11th.

There are some very peculiar parallels between me and Lilian Baylis, who was at The Old Vic between 1898–1937 (running it solely from 1912), besides my having been here for only five years shy of her record. It's odd that Lilian was born a week after me in our respective years, both of us in the month of May. Lilian died in November 1937, the date a week after I began here in November 1986. I've always found that spooky. I do conclude that after all the things that have happened over the years, such as management changes, an ownership change, Artistic Directors coming and going, and latterly virus mutations, I'm still here and that (as Mr Sondheim wrote) it's the bricks and mortar of the place that keep me happily imprisoned. It seems almost as if fate drew me here those years ago, if you believe that old rubbish, and anyway, one must not be complacent because, as for tomorrow, well, who knows? (as Mr Fierstein wrote). I'm very proud of the old girl (if we're allowed to differentiate these days) at 203 years old and still going. I'll not make it to that age but will slide off my perch still doing what I have a passion for. A little discombobulating for the next occupant of the seat, but hey, that's the way of the world.

As for being one of longest serving stage door keepers, well, I never think about it, one never likes to be reminded of one's age. Although I suppose it's kind of neat really!

Ned Seago

INTRODUCTION

All the world's a stage,
And all the men and women merely players;
They have their exits and their entrances…
and their stage doors.

In 2020, for the first time in centuries, there were no theatres open in London.

As two actors who felt that they had lost their homes away from home, we turned to another form of art that could survive the pandemic - photography. *Exeunt - The Stage Door Project* is a collection of memories - images by us and words by theatre luminaries you know and love - brought together to document the effects of the coronavirus pandemic on London's West End.

Who in this industry doesn't dream of walking through the theatrical pearly gates, of feeling the chaos of London's streets being replaced by the ethereal calm of backstage preparations, of gently being reminded to sign in (and out) by the angels at the door?

This book is a tribute to the magical experience that occurs at the stage door. But most of all, it's a celebration of the legendary places, the industry professionals and the countless audience members who weathered the storm together.

Ours is a book to celebrate what we endured together.

All of us.

Lloyd McDonagh & Salvatore Scarpa

THE STAGE DOOR PROJECT

Ernie Davis was stage doorman at The Old Vic when I was there in 1960 when we did *She Stoops to Conquer* with Tommy Steele. Tommy received a letter from a fan asking him to sing 'Little White Bull' during the show that night as he was attending with an elderly relation!! Ernie loved the letter so much he asked Tommy if he could keep it... and he did. Stage doormen are rare and marvellous people.

Dame Judi Dench

As a Director, it is not often that I enter through a stage door. There is usually a lonely route to the auditorium through front of house which delivers me straight to my makeshift desk. Directors tend to slip into a theatre alone as actors throng and giggle their way to dressing rooms filled with cards and keepsakes, charms and sweet smells. So, when I think of stage doors, I think of times when I am off duty, anonymous and relaxingly not in charge; a stage door Johnnie if you like! My partner works in the theatre and it is a great joy for me to go and meet him from work; usually at The Old Vic in London. I love to loiter opposite the stage door in the knowledge that he will soon appear. It is at these times, stood in the road, basking in the warmth of the neon that I remember the fairy dust that theatre sprinkles onto our lives. The excitement of not knowing who will pop out of that magic door is intoxicating; it could be a wardrobe assistant, a star or the love of my life. The stage door is a gateway to such electric endeavour, a world of colour, surprise, possibility and potential. This door is the gateway to all I love and all I believe in – and I tingle with a humble sense of gratitude that I am lucky enough to be part of it. Then Simon appears in a chaos of bags and banter with the stage door keeper – and all my dreams come true at once. I get to whisk him to a warm bar for a debrief, decompress and a slow digestion of the day's events. The memory of these nights, this peek into the ephemeral wonder of the telling of stories, has a sweet neon glow and a melancholic sense of loss. When we come back, will the magnificent, messy, mysterious chaos of humanity return? I hope with my whole tired heart that it will.

Emma Rice

In the late 80s, the old stage door outside light was nicked. I rounded the corner of Webber Street and noticed the globe had gone, and when the LX department arrived to work I asked if they were working on it. No they were not, in fact they hadn't seen it was gone. Whoever made away with it had sawn through the swan-neck bracket and wiring. We never discovered who or why.

One morning in 1988 I arrived for work to find the whole of the stage door interior and staircases awash. At that time the stairs were carpeted and the aroma of damp, old, and not necessarily pristine carpet is certainly not to be sniffed at. It stank! Somebody, again we never found out who, had broken the above dressing room window and delivered an incendiary device. The sprinkler system had done its work and damage. Structurally this was insignificant, but we've never had carpeted stairways since.

In 2001, a show called *Over the Moon* was rehearsing with us before doing a short tour and then returning to our stage. On one particular afternoon there was no rehearsing done. Around the old radio I then had (before we hit the 20th century at the Vic with a stage door computer) were gathered Joan Collins, Ray Cooney (director), Moira Lister and Frank Langella, all listening to news from New York. The date was September 11th.

There are some very peculiar parallels between me and Lilian Baylis, who was at The Old Vic between 1898–1937 (running it solely from 1912), besides my having been here for only five years shy of her record. It's odd that Lilian was born a week after me in our respective years, both of us in the month of May. Lilian died in November 1937, the date a week after I began here in November 1986. I've always found that spooky. I do conclude that after all the things that have happened over the years, such as management changes, an ownership change, Artistic Directors coming and going, and latterly virus mutations, I'm still here and that (as Mr Sondheim wrote) it's the bricks and mortar of the place that keep me happily imprisoned. It seems almost as if fate drew me here those years ago, if you believe that old rubbish, and anyway, one must not be complacent because, as for tomorrow, well, who knows? (as Mr Fierstein wrote). I'm very proud of the old girl (if we're allowed to differentiate these days) at 203 years old and still going. I'll not make it to that age but will slide off my perch still doing what I have a passion for. A little discombobulating for the next occupant of the seat, but hey, that's the way of the world.

As for being one of longest serving stage door keepers, well, I never think about it, one never likes to be reminded of one's age. Although I suppose it's kind of neat really!

Ned Seago

The Old Vic Theatre

Almost without exception, stage doors are poky little places, presided over by a sedentary figure with whom one exchanges a few cheery words and then moves on into the theatre itself. They are transitional spaces of no great inherent interest. As an actor one signs oneself in and then swiftly proceeds on to the dressing room, where one will spend a great deal of time, unless it's a one–man show, and even then, in that private space, time before, during and after the show is of crucial psychological importance.

The stage door hardly figures at all. And yet it is there, in that mundane, functional little space, that the crucial transition occurs in which you receive a sort of odd invisible coating that enables you to undertake the crucial transition from the you that exists in the real world to the you that will give yourself over to a whole other identity, in which your mind, your heart and your body will be infused with other thoughts, other sensations, other needs.

The stage door is like the hole down which Alice falls into Wonderland, the portal of the space ship which one enters into the fourth dimension, the circle of fire through which Siegfried passes to claim Brünnhilde, Dr Who's phone box. Pass through the stage door and you have begun the journey from which there can be no turning back until you have completed what you came to do. And when you reverse the process at the end of the show, and sign yourself out, you re-emerge as a regular member of the human race, John Citizen again, cleansed of that spooky stuff, that transforming ectoplasm that adhered to you on your way in.

It is at the stage door that you shed it.

Simon Callow

I'm fascinated by the transiency of theatres. Stories, like nomads, settle for a short while then pick up sticks, leaving space for the next. And to me, an audience does the same thing. Each night a new body, a different voice, a whole other perspective goes on a journey with those of us on stage. A silent bystander but the last and most important piece of the puzzle. And the stage door is where the two finally get to meet. After going through so much together. Living, breathing, laughing, crying, loving together. It's the portal that bleeds fantasy and reality. For now, they are vacant. Calm. But the winds have hopefully changed direction. See you soon, old friend.

John McCrea

The Apollo Theatre

The Novello Theatre

There's something so exciting about walking through a stage door. You think of all the amazing creatives that have stepped through those doors through the years. You think of all the incredible staff that keep the theatre going. It always feels like you are walking into a world of possibilities that's never happened before and will never happen again.

Diane Page

Arriving at Stage Door is always a magical experience. I think signing into the building every day, getting to know the person on the door, all adds to the way working in theatre makes you feel part of a close-knit family.

There's great excitement attached to the stage door and the constant announcements over the tannoy that 'a parcel has arrived for Mr Such and Such' or 'Flowers at Stage Door for Dressing Room One'.

And then, of course, when the relief and adrenaline is rushing through your veins having just finished a performance, there is the nightly theatre ritual of people 'coming round'. This is when guests arrive at Stage Door and are brought to the dressing rooms of the actors that they know. The enjoyment of seeing friends and (more importantly) them telling you that you are definitely the best one in it, is one of the great nightly treats of any theatrical run.

Theatres transport you to other worlds, both as an audience member and also if you're part of the crew that conspire to create that magical journey. Backstage is a thrilling place to hang out; as is the green room and the auditorium itself when spending night after night lolling in the stalls during long and arduous technical rehearsals.

All these delights await when you enter the building via... Stage Door.

Reece Shearsmith

The theatres in the West End are closed. They stand dark and forsaken, waiting for society to bring them back to life again. If you walk around the corner, or down the alley a few yards away, or go round the block to the back of the building, you will find the stage doors. The entrance for performers of all kinds to enter the building and reach their dressing rooms, where they will prepare to perform the night's entertainment. These too stand silent now, their doors firmly shut against the world. So many talented people – from actors, singers and dancers, to writers, directors and producers, to dressers, costume people and cleaners – have passed through these doors. Wigs and costume jewellery, flowers, presents and champagne are carried through them into the world where magic, laughter, tears, sadness, joy flow freely. Now they wait, as we all do, for the world to recover from this Covid nightmare so that they may open their doors once more and welcome back their life blood… Their people.

Anita Dobson

One of the great privileges of my life has been visiting my dad at various stage doors. After taking a lengthy theatrical sabbatical, my first experience of this was at the Tricycle, where he was brilliant in a play I saw eleven times. I waited each time with giggly pride at their modest version of a stage door, which led straight into the bar, for him to come out. Then, at the Lyric, where he starred in his own play, *Ghost Stories*, I would creep out of their almost invisible stage door at beginners, and watch him start the show from an auditorium doorway. Later on, following their West End transfer, I'd walk from my school in Marylebone to the Duke of York's, to hang out with him most days. You could regularly catch me at Cafe Koha, having a mint tea and gazing at the Wyndham's stage door in anticipation of the end of his *Abigail's Party* matinée, so he could join me for an early pre-show dinner. Or at the same theatre soon after for *Hangmen*, which starred both Dad and an ex-boyfriend, resulting in me clarifying on entry: 'I'm here to see Dad' or 'I'm here to see Joe' and then a ceremonial 'I know, what are the chances!?' if it was someone new on the door! More recently, dropping a bag of 100 Brick Lane bagels at the Menier stage door for the *Fiddler on the Roof* press night, foreseeing a transfer, bringing with it the comfort of knowing Dad's behind a door in the West End, meaning I have a little slice of home if I'm in town, in the form of fatherly comfort, or the nuts he always keeps stocked up for me in his room. And then, as expected, *Fiddler* at the Playhouse, visiting regularly, as it was a tight fifteen-minute walk from my front door to his temporary back door, often finding my mum already there doing a jigsaw, or my brother, having a natter. Always listening, with great pride, as the person manning the door remarked on what a close family we were, how gorgeous it was that we spent so much time together, how they'd never known another actor's family like it. And lastly, the feeling of pride I had being biologically linked to this man, leaving that stage door with him at the end of the show, when fans gathered outside in awe of the performance he had given, or the hilarity of the time a nervous Mum shouted 'do you want my panties?' as we left together, something that is now infamous in our family. It is almost impossible to quantify the fulfilment I feel, leaving a stage door after I have performed, to see my dad waiting for me on the other side, after so many years of entering stage doors to visit him. The doors that have bookmarked my life. The doors that have shaped me into the person, and actor, I am today.

Macy Nyman

The Playhouse Theatre

I was introduced to my first stage door at the age of fourteen. It was the loading dock entrance to my high-school auditorium and the gateway to… my life.

Unbeknownst to me then, this and each subsequent stage door would become, not just for me but for many lucky enough or brave enough to enter, the portal to a world of endless adventure and discoveries of which we were yet incapable of dreaming.

This first stage door for me led to an awakening and the beginning of a lifetime spent grappling with art, skill, technique, taste, patience, exhaustion, bliss, disappointment, success, self, friendship, love, loss and life.

It's true, this same grappling might have taken place in some other field or in any other place of work. But, oh, there is nothing so special as the world backstage. There's a magic that exists only here and a depth of experience unlike anywhere else.

Today, forty-six years later, as these doorways that have been closed and silent for more than a year slowly come back to life, my step still quickens and my heart still beats faster as I approach. I shush the voice of doubt and summon what courage I need as I scan the building, excitedly, impatiently, searching for the words that will once again welcome me home: Stage Door.

David Bedella

THE DARKENED STILLNESS OF A SMALL FRAME
THE UNASSUMING ILLUMINATION ABOVE ITS TWO WORDS
THE INVITATION TO ENTER
AN OPENING INTO ETERNITY…

How we long to see the magic behind those doors, where enter and exit the magic-makers, who spin enchanted tales and take us to another world. Magic-makers who tell us stories, teach us imagination, charm us and captivate us, spun in tears of joy and laughter, of pain and sorrow, of defeat and victory, of despair and hope; all through the stillness of a small frame… into eternal life.

And when we say our 'well dones' and our 'goodnights', slipping away into the quiet of the night, the stage door is never far from sight.

Kwong Loke

STAGE DOOR

The Shaftesbury Theatre

Stage doors are wonderful places! Whatever is going on in your life or is happening in the world seems to disappear the moment you step through it. The moment the stage door keeper says 'hello', you are carried off to a different world. I have to say, it is one of the greatest feelings I've ever felt. I can't wait to feel it again!

Luke Giles

It took me some years to understand fully what a stage door really is. I think I initially saw it as the gateway to where the 'real work' happens. And of course it is that – behind every stage door is a labyrinth of walkways leading to the countless doors behind which magic takes place…

But a stage door is something much bigger; it is the threshold between the real world and the make-believe. The place where the performer's veil lifts and they stand eye to eye with the audience who, whether or not they like it, are the reason for our existence.

My chief moment of realisation came on my first commercial job, a number-one tour of *The Vagina Monologues*. I was in esteemed company, sharing a stage with national treasure Linda Robson, and national treasure-in-waiting (soon to become *Downton Abbey*'s Mrs Patmore) Lesley Nicol.

In a Damascene moment at one venue we visited: my track included the party piece, 'Reclaiming Cunt' (a spicy monologue usually saved for the intrepid juve) which involves seducing/cajoling/whipping the audience into a frenzy enough to get them all screaming the 'C' word back at you. Things were not helped by the fact that my Catholic Indian mother was in the audience that night. All I could think about was the unbearable awfulness of faking an orgasm in front of her.

I should add that she is completely wonderful, my mum, and was moved to genuine tears by the whole *VM* experience. After giving her a backstage tour, we found two young British South Asian women waiting at Stage Door. They had stayed long after Linda's troupe had left to tell me how much it meant to them, seeing someone who looked like them up there, being so liberated and strong.

I had always wanted to make theatre for a reason, and that day those ladies articulated it for me. I cannot begin to express how much it meant to me that they felt that, and stayed on at the stage door to say it.

Stephanie Street

The Apollo Victoria Theatre

His picture was all over my bedroom walls. I had studied his every move in the film of *Romeo and Juliet*. The big treat of the year was being taken to see him live at Covent Garden. And now I was off to meet him.

Back in 1985 I was in a production of *The Possessed* that started at the Almeida and then went on a European tour. The play was conceived by the renowned Russian director Yuri Lyubimov and when it hit the Odéon in Paris, *le tout emigré monde Russe* turned out to see it – including Rudolf Nureyev.

Noticing my ecstatic reaction to his presence in the audience, our company manager, who happened also to be the company manager for Nureyev's summer season at the Coliseum in London, suggested I might like to watch his *Swan Lake* from the wings in June. When June came around she was true to her word. She told me she had had to clear it with Rudi himself, reminding him of my performance in Paris, and I apparently passed the test.

So on a beautiful warm June evening I rocked up at this stage door dressed in black (as instructed) and was taken to prompt corner to wait. I could see him warming up on stage. I didn't breathe. He asked to meet me. I dropped my bag and crept into his sphere. He cross-examined me about Lyubimov and asked what I thought of Solzhenitsyn. I wanted to say 'I have worshipped you since I was 11 and your genius inspired me to act'; instead I behaved with a sort of paralysed cool.

But later, watching that familiar entrance to that familiar Tchaikovsky score, I wept in the safety of the darkness. Now and then he would come off into the wings, drink some water, put on his leg-warmers, and several times he spoke to me or cracked a joke; 'This old cow needs a trampoline'.

When I went to his dressing room afterwards to thank him and to say it was wonderful, he sort of scoffed as if to say, 'If you thought that was wonderful you're a fool.' I wanted to say 'I saw you at your peak and I know your leaping days are over but that's not the point. This had been the most wondrous, extraordinary, magical evening of my life'. I didn't say any of that…

I floated out of the stage door and into the warm, still light London evening, telling my younger self, 'You get to meet him in the end'.

Dame Harriet Walter

The London Coliseum

I remember sitting outside Stage Door at The Duke of York's when I was working as Associate Director on a West End transfer. We'd just taken a break from a very stressful technical rehearsal and I was having five minutes on the bench outside under the fairy lights which were always lit there in the evenings. One of our producers joined me and we joked about the difficult rehearsal we'd all just experienced. As she rose to head back in, she paused and said 'I'm very impressed with you, I'm sure we'll see you back here one day.' I smiled and followed her back through the door and onto stage to resume rehearsals. Two years later I was back under those fairy lights laughing with the very same producer. I was in technical rehearsals for another West End transfer, this time my own production, a version of *Summer and Smoke* which we were moving from the Almeida Theatre. Having my own show at the beautiful Duke of York's was a privilege I will never forget, and the memory of it will always hold images of the bench, fairy lights and 'Stage Door' lantern that hover round the back of the theatre. Walking through that stage door every day felt like coming home. I hope I get a third time there.

Rebecca Frecknall

The theatre is a place of Youth.
I say that
Not just because I'm young
(That'll fade, some day)
But, because
Everyone who walks through those doors
Crossing the threshold
where Imagination becomes Reality
On entry
Immediately
becomes a Child.
Not just the actors, everyone.
Mildly managed mischief
From the half to curtain call
Toddlers.
In Search Of
Well,
Life.
It's like a nightclub.
The arts' best kept secret.
The doors shut
The lights go out
anything can happen.
Innovation, renovation.
Little do we know,
We're creating History.
Every time we walk through that square called Stage Door.

David Jonsson

The Duke of York's Theatre

For us people working in theatre, the stage door is the back of the wardrobe in *The Lion, the Witch and the Wardrobe* – it is a portal into our Narnia, a fantastical world that only we can access. Every stage door keeper I've ever known has been a brilliant combination of bouncer – 'If your name's not down you're not coming in!' – and maître d'hôtel, welcoming us in and showing us to our rooms. Fans can wait outside in anxious queues for autographs and selfies with their idols – but they'll never get past these gatekeepers. Only those who work in the building will ever be allowed in. Often tucked down little alleys or back streets, mostly grubby, sometimes offering shelter from the elements for the homeless, stage doors are not the glamorous access points most people imagine – but they are nevertheless portals of privilege. Those of us who get to go through them are lucky. We yearn for that pass, that nod in, for our name to be on the list. It's my hope that, coming out of this dark period for live theatre, we see more diverse entries through these doors – theatre stage doors should be welcoming more Black workers, more women, more older women, more disabled workers, more working-class people across all these intersections. For those who cross the threshold of the stage door get to tell the stories – and whoever tells the stories is part of the narrative our culture writes.

Jackie Clune

As a child, I was always fascinated walking past the stage door of a theatre – that mysterious portal into a world behind the scenes. I'll never forget the overwhelming feeling of excitement stepping through the stage door of The Theatre Royal Drury Lane to take part in work experience on the then playing *Miss Saigon*. What an experience that was! I was in awe of the stagecraft I witnessed. Those few steps began a journey propelling me toward my career as a lighting designer. I was fortunate to return many years later to light the Olivier Awards. Whilst the decor may have changed, the atmosphere remained and immediately all those emotions returned. No matter what or where the production may be, this excitement never fades. Long may I have the privilege to step through those magical doors.

Ben Cracknell

Theatre Royal Drury Lane

The Stage Door; a love letter.

All stage doors smell the same – whether they're large or small or modern or shabby. They all whiff of 60% church, 25% printing press, 10% bleach and 5% adrenalin. They're like Bilbo Baggins' hideaway – but with a mini kettle and an oversized cork notice board. Invariably there'll be a tiny black and white CCTV set with an image screen burned in that hasn't changed since 1977. No doubt there will also be eleventy billion cardboard boxes stacked strategically around the entrance containing the over order of that week's show's programmes. There will be a fire signing-in book with various names scrawled onto its inky leaves and next to it a recently chewed biro gaffer-taped to a waxy bit of blue string to preclude any light-fingered turns from nicking it. Oh, and God help you if you forget to sign yourself out!

Which brings us on to the stage door keepers themselves. A select group of individuals with a unique set of certain skills. They are a constant contradiction; attentive but uninterested, warm yet distant, absent but yet oh so present. They will have forgotten more about the comings and goings of that theatre than any actor, accountant or architect could ever know. To be a fully paid-up member of the Stage Door Keepers' Club, however, they must be doing at least one of the following four things as you arrive at their desk: 1. Knitting, 2. Stuffing an envelope, 3. Reading a book or 4. Eating. (I once saw Kirsty, the keeper at Bath's Theatre Royal, do all four at once!) Oh! And they'll never be new to the job. Ask any of them how long they've worked there, and their answer will literally be in its hundreds if not thousands of years.

I've been lucky enough to pass through quite a few in my life. As a young actor, I even got to work at one in between gigs. I looked after the door of Brighton's Theatre Royal. For a theatre obsessive like me, it was almost too exciting to get to perch on an old bar stool behind a makeshift pull-down desk, meeting and greeting different actors each week before they trod the boards as Hamlet, Henry or Havisham. I never had the nerve to try and engage in conversations with any of them but I still got a thrill passing over their dressing room key as they buffaloed through the shabby red door off Brighton's salty Bond St. I remember one actor being the epitome of swash, buckle and swag as he bounced through eight times a week. I was so in awe of his actorishness that I'd regularly drop my knitting! I won't use his real name – let's call him Higel Navers. Five minutes before curtain down every evening, his driver would pull up outside the back door. He would get out and enter carrying a large Waterford crystal whisky glass. He'd place it gently on my desk and then pour in two generous fingers of Glenlivet. He would leave it there and then go back outside to the car and start the engine. Moments later, Navers would mince off stage, still wearing white face make-up and full costume of periwig and breeches, through to the back of the theatre, past the desk, pick up the Scotch without stopping and duck straight out and into his waiting Jag. He would then growl off back to London to the sound of the audience still applauding and with hollers of 'Bravo!' singing from the stalls. My job for the rest of the evening would be to placate the baying crowd of fans who'd ran around in search of an autograph. They found it very difficult to accept that he'd already left the building some minutes earlier.

But here's the thing; stage doors are invaluable. The first thing opened in the morning and the last one locked at night. As important and as synonymous to the realm of the theatre as the box office or the interval gin and tonic. Come the end of the world, they will be one of the few survivors – just an apocalyptic tundra containing only them, cockroaches and the Rolling Stones. A secretive backstage world of gossip, laughter and love. A den of 'in Equity' if you will. Would that those wooden frames of the two score back doors that make up London's West End could talk – could you imagine the tattle? From Kidman to Kean, Daniels Craig, Radcliffe and Day-Lewis; the plagues, pandemics, pestilence and paparazzi; that seven-foot-tall portal into and out of the most magical arena of the arts has seen it all.

Just don't forget to sign out as you leave.

Richard Sutton

The Prince of Wales Thea

I remember how petrified I felt walking through The National Theatre's stage door for the first time in my life to audition for *Tartuffe* on Friday 23rd November 2018. This was the biggest theatre role I had auditioned for, and my nerves were through the roof, and I couldn't stop shaking. After convincing myself I just performed the worst acting in front of the Director and Casting Director, I actually just cried outside the stage door because I was most certain I blew it.

On Wednesday 2nd January 2019, I walked through The National Theatre's stage door for the second time, for the first day of rehearsals for *Tartuffe*. This time, the tears were 'I did it'.

Adeyinka Akinrinade

National Theatre. HELEN McCRORY!

Threepenny Opera was on the same time as *Deep Blue Sea* at The National. And my track meant that at a certain point in a quick change, I always bumped into Helen. And it was like that for leading up to press night.

Helen is cordial and magnanimous of spirit. It was always a nod and smile, even though I could sense she was in the zone.

Anyway, cut to press night. We bump into each other at Stage Door. She's got a comical amount of flowers, and we have a little giggle about it.

Helen McCrory sighs 'press night'.
Me (twat), 'don't be shit, babe'.

She burst out laughing, and I was mortified. In my clown brain, because we'd been bumping into each other so much, I didn't see Helen McCrory, I saw a theatre buddy and was way too colloquial. We all had a chuckle at Stage Door. From then on, every time we crossed, when our shows were on, she would look at me and chuckle like, this absolute clown told me to not be shit. HELEN McCRORY! Haha.

She is a wonder of an actress and this exchange could only have happened at The National Theatre's stage door. Magic.

Le Gateau Chocolat

One of my favourite places in the world – one that makes me feel most at home – is the National Theatre stage door. When I first walked back through that entrance – the first time I went back into a theatre in that hiatus between lockdowns – the security guards – the familiarity – the sense of home – it made me cry.

It's the way into the hidden world where the unseen live – those thousands of arts workers who make it all happen that the audience never see. The lampies, the follow-spot operators, the dressers, the actors, the carpenters, the wigs department – from producers and stars to cleaning staff and firemen – we all go through that door. It's our portal to the world we miss so much. Our way in…

Always by the bins. A whiff of recycling and decayed glamour. Bonkers fans outside. Doors that are usually too small to get your Brompton fold-up bike through. The madness of signing in and out. The piles of cards and deliveries.

Stage door keepers are the heart of the building – at other times the gatekeepers.

Paule Constable

Stage Door

The National Theatre

…It never ever gets old or tired for me: signing in and the mundane rituals; the idle chit-chat; the banter; the relationships and connections that build up gradually over months and years with colleagues front of house; the slow, steady stream of fellow players and dreamers and mischief-makers and just good, decent hard-working professionals doing their job, coming and going. I still get giddy even now – nearly thirty years down the line of making my living doing the thing I love – at the thought that I get to walk through those magical, mysterious stage doors. A portal into another secret, sacred world; where perhaps, for just a few hours, everything can be just a little bit perfect. But really and truly? When I look at them, I remember a 17-year-old on the other side of the world, several lifetimes ago, with a wild, wild dream that one day he too would pass through the doors into a world of dreams. And I remind a care-worn, battle-hardened teller of tales to never forget to honour that kid because he made it to the other side; so it is possible. Wherever there's a door, it's possible…

Lucian Msamati

After all this time, my heartbeat awakens at Stage Door.
Magic and mystique lie behind.
Like Wonka's Chocolate Factory, you can't see the secrets being cooked.
They are always olfactorily particular. Each with its own specific aroma.
Greasepaint is still apparent despite years of neglect, stale seventies smoke, sweat, glue, coffee.

Perfect for all dramatic entrances and exits.
Power and jealousy play a part.
Years as a child, of access denied.
Now, where you can only stand and wait, I have free passage.
My right to roam.
Turn on the mirror lights, turn down the tannoy.
Breathe.
That feeling again.
The very essence of Home.

Adrian Scarborough

The Criterion Theatre

I was sorry that I never met Miriam Barron, stage door keeper at the Fortune Theatre for, oh, 15 years or more; and by all accounts a warm and wonderful personality who cared deeply for her charges, staff, cast and crew, all equally.

The Fortune, dwarfed by the Theatre Royal on the other side of the road, is a narrow building, built in the 1920s on the site of a pub bombed in the First World War. The stage door is on an alley, off Russell St, and the keeper's room is cosy and surprisingly spacious, compared with some of the poky nooks in other West End theatres. From there a narrow staircase goes down to the stage, or the other way winds up to the green room, dressing rooms and offices above. From the dressing rooms you can see, over the high wall on the opposite side of the alley, a playground, built on the site of a plague pit.

When I first worked there, in *Woman in Black*, in 2011, we had a rota of door keepers, everyone welcoming and helpful. There was Lele, an Italian with an irrepressible optimism and a beaming smile. Chatting with him was always a joy, even though I know nothing about football or Lambrettas. And when we had guests who came round for a glass of wine after the show, he always gave us far, far more than the allotted 20 minutes to clear out – and sometimes he'd bolt the stage door and come and join us.

Dan Whelan was quieter, a sensitive and thoughtful fellow. How do you spend your time when the show is on? I asked him. I'm writing a novel, he replied. And the book, *Box of Demons* was later published, with illustrations by Chris Riddell.

Tomisin Adjepu must be, by far, the best-dressed stage door keeper ever. A handsome Nigerian, he was always immaculately dressed in a three-piece suit and tie. He is now a very successful, award-winning film maker.

Long live the stage door keeper!

David Acton

I hope I never take for granted the excitement of a stage door. Feeling very briefly like a rock star whilst clutching a Pret sandwich for breakfast (at 2pm), checking post that will almost certainly not be for you and ticking in before stage management notice you are late are all part and parcel of the job, and made better by that pollution-stained light box sign. It gives me a wee buzz of excitement. And yes, I will still linger when walking past the crowd formed to see who's signing that night.

Natalie Law

The Fortune Theatre

Down dim cobbled streets of the west,
A shadow looms over the arches,
An entrance silently sleeping,
Whilst a flicker fights back the darkness.

These empty halls of rebellion,
An echo of times not so past,
Ushered through doors soon thrown open,
A deafening silence not meant to last.

Near all the lights are extinguished.
Countless wings have been plucked.
Threads lay unravelled and broken,
On boards, unplugged and untouched.

Memories were born here,
Ambitions were shaped.
Our lives and our stories,
Behind red and gold drapes.

The thunderous clap in the distance,
The skilled and brave answer the call,
The reprisal will soon be at hand, friends,
Our final curtain shall never fall.

Gordon Millar

Stage Door is like the gateway to the magic. That place between fantasy and reality.
It is that moment when you're not quite your character on stage, but nor are you
completely yourself.

I've had some of the most humbling and touching moments at Stage Door. I find it
especially beautiful when young performers meet you with tears in their eyes and
hope in their hearts because they can see themselves in you. There is that moment
of connection, as though you're their dream personified, and that in turn gives
me energy and hope to keep pushing and progressing. It's an extremely unique
exchange of energy, one that at first feels strange, but moments like that are the
reason I always try and come out after a show and greet the audience. Because you
never know who is waiting for you, who you can inspire just by saying hello with a
little eye contact, or who could be the next push or motivation you need to perform
your next show.

Leanne Robinson

The Peacock Theatre

I've always found stage doors the most wonderfully mysterious places. Like doorways to a world that straddle reality and fantasy. Even now my pulse quickens at the opening of a stage door, as I wait outside to meet a friend or simply walk past one. I'm always intrigued to see who or what comes out and find it impossible not to try and steal a glance inside to see what secrets it holds. When I enter or exit a stage door where I'm working, I feel the most immense sense of pride that someone might be watching, feeling that same sense of intrigue as I step through. That they might like to know things that I know, and see what I'm about to see or have just seen.

Stage doors make the most normal people seem utterly fascinating.

Thomas Aldridge

Near the end of Shaftesbury Avenue, as it corners into Charing Cross Road, sits the magnificent Palace Theatre. An iconic theatre building which, in my early years in London as a Central St Martins Art Student, was the building that housed *Les Misérables*.

I'd often pass it after college going into Soho or Chinatown for food with friends, just as all the lights of the theatres dotted down Shaftesbury Avenue would start to ping on, signalling the beginning of Theatreland's storytelling for the evening.

The whole area was always so full of life, people and the buzz of a good night out. And somehow, if arriving from the Cambridge Circus, The Palace Theatre, with its elaborate frontage and prominent position, felt almost like the grand entrance gate to the visceral and magical world of the streets behind.

Many shows later The Palace Theatre now houses *Harry Potter and the Cursed Child*, which I was invited into as costume designer for the show.

Walking up Shaftesbury Avenue from the Piccadilly Circus early in the morning, coffee in hand, the hum, banging and clattering of piles of glass bottles as the bin men and street cleaners start their day, I am beginning the first day of the tech on the show.

As I arrive at the junction to Greek Street, I see the stage door for the theatre for the first time. I'd never really noticed it all those years before. So different from the front. It's a small humble-looking double door made of wood with two average-sized square windows sitting high within it. Unassuming and unrevealing of the life beyond other than the brilliant carved stone lintel on top, which reads:

'Palace Theatre Stage Entrance. The world's greatest artistes have passed and will pass through these doors.'

This stage door lintel is such a welcoming gesture to all the eco-system of theatre artists that have passed, do pass and will pass through these doors. The tribes of people that go into making any show.

By being placed so deliberately above this simple stage door portal, it seems to acknowledge with elegance the magic of the everyday work, collaboration, play and hard grit of the teams who pass through these doors. The beauty of the backstage world elevated into art and celebrating all the various artists that combine to make theatre in this country world class.

A simple door with a long legacy and big future aspirations. I love that.

Katrina Lindsay

The Palace Theatre

Shakespeare's Globe

I remember the first time I stepped out onto the Globe stage. I had left drama school early to perform in my first professional role as Hiti in *Pitcairn* by Richard Bean. It was a feeling I'll never forget and have rarely shared as it was so personal and almost indescribable. As I made my entrance, I was dazzled and mesmerised by the light coming from the galleries; the air was thick with expectation and wonder. I felt the life and energy of all who had trod those boards coursing through my veins. And, as I opened my mouth to utter my opening lines, it was as though something else took over. A higher power, and I was elevated to a different realm. I've never felt anything quite like it. It truly felt like a piece of heaven on earth.

On my journey to the theatre, I normally have my music on getting me into my zone. Either songs that remind me of who I am, or songs that pump me up in some way. When I go through that stage door it's game time. I feel like a sportsman entering the arena, focused and ready.

Eben Figueiredo

Working on the technical side of things often means doing very long hours, so often the stage door keeper is the first person you see at around 08:45 and the last person you see at 22:15. The difference they can make to your day is huge. If they're bright and fun, it sets you up nicely and if they let you know as soon as the delivery you're desperately waiting for arrives, it can mean the difference between an irate director and a calm one. However, if they let random people into the theatre who are looking for a totally different building (actually happened), it can be frustrating and hazardous. And, frankly, Stage Door is my first port of call if I'm stuck on a crossword clue. Whilst always giving the show my full attention, of course.

Andy Taylor

The definition of the 'stage door' is an actors' and workmen's entrance from the street to the area of a theatre behind the stage, but it is so much more than that. The stage door is a magical place, where dreams become reality. To see a show with your favourite actors and then be able to catch them at the stage door after, take a picture, sign a programme, have a hug, is so special! But from the actors' point of view, we get to meet the people who we have shared this joint experience with, we get to hear directly from them what they thought of the show and go beyond the audience's collective clap and hear the real stories of what theatre really means to them and how it has touched and changed their lives. I think theatre and live art is more powerful than we know, and I'm so proud to be a small part of it.

Aimie Atkinson

My first professional acting job was playing Albert in the West End production of *War Horse*. It was at the Gillian Lynne Theatre – then the New London Theatre – a hulking great concrete and steel construction on Drury Lane. The stage door is like a prison entry system, with huge gates and electrical entry systems. But to me it was like a portal to a magical world. Each day, when I stepped off the streets of London and signed my name on the doorkeeper's register, it was the first step towards that night's performance. It marked the border between daily life and the build-up to the evening's act of creation.

Over the last ten years, I've been lucky enough to pass through many more stage doors, all of them magical portals to a world of romance, performance, hilarity and naughtiness. The fun, the jokes, the pranks and the gossip all await on the other side of the stage door. They are Rubicons, beyond which you are no longer your sensible, adult self.

Stage doors are like tardises or the entrance to Diagon Alley: most people's eyes slip right past them. But, if you know what you're looking for, you'll spot them. To those of us who have been lucky enough to pass through them – they are sacred.

Jack Holden

The Gillian Lynne Theatre

It must have been around 1989 when I walked through my first stage door. I was performing in Patricia Mulholland's *Irish Ballets*. It helped that it meant getting out of school early, but I still remember the feeling that it was a true privilege. A privilege that I was allowed to step through this magic portal into another world, leaving behind the mundanity of the real world (or unfortunately not-so-mundane 1980s Belfast) and entering a dreamland. I still feel that way. Every single time I step through a stage door, I feel privileged and can't believe I'm allowed to do it.

Laura Donnelly

When I was seven years old it was the small exit where I saw Fairies, Dames and the Pied Piper come into the outside world. There was a fire alarm at the Theatr Clwyd rock-n-roll pantomime and we children were all excitedly and nervously ushered out into the car park. We were expecting to see gigantic flames licking at the roof any second (it turns out there was just too much Elnett hairspray used in the dressing rooms). Then as we waited under the Welsh sky, out of a small and nondescript metal door came the cast, dressed in glitter and smiles and shimmering wings, with their instruments still in their adult hands. It seemed as though we'd all gone from Narnia back into the wardrobe, and suddenly these rock stars existed in our world too! Outside in the fresh air! I'll never forget the feeling of possibility and excitement seeing them there in the daylight.

Then a few years later, that same stage door welcomed me for my first professional job. My name was then on the list tucked into the clipboard, the dangling biro tied to a string. That same car park where I witnessed the magic was now where I parked my Clio (Rio was her name, if you're asking).

When I moved to London and worked at the Gielgud Theatre in the West End, the stage door was the border of Soho and its sparkling bars, and 1980s rural Ireland. The noise stopped from Rupert Street and became the calling of Beginners. On sunny days, pints were being drunk across the road while we were drinking Bushmills (well, water with some gravy granules) in a kitchen cottage. The juxtaposition between those two worlds was enormous and beautiful.

And the keepers of that door were just as important as the border itself. Always there to chat to and give you the news. Literally, one time, a shoulder to cry on. Answerer of all the questions: 'Which team of children do we have on tonight?' 'Do you know whether the Korean chicken place down the road does takeaway? I've only got twenty minutes before we start the evening show,' and 'Can we stay on a bit later tonight because it's St Patrick's Day and we're planning on squeezing all thirty of us into Dressing Room 9 to drink Guinness?'

The stage door. It's always an adventure when you step through it. A border from the present into boundless possibilities.

Laurie Kynaston

I miss stage doors. When I walk through them I feel like I'm escaping into a magical world. Then, when I walk back out, the real world feels just a bit more magical. It's a wonderful portal that never fails to give me new perspectives on the worlds on either side of it.

Abraham Popoola

The Gielgud Theatre

Trafalgar Studios is a slightly cramped, concrete municipal backstage. The stage door is a classic of the period and directly anterior to the front of house. The roof is a superb space.

I was in my second year at Drama Centre when I saw a play at the King's Head called *Mr Joyce is Leaving Paris*. It was brilliant, the first half was a two-hander and Jim Norton played Stanislaus (Stanny), James' long-suffering brother. I remember walking into the sodium glare of Upper St and telling my girlfriend (Annie) 'That's the actor I want to be'. Years later I played Stanny at the Traverse.

Forward some decades, I did several tours of Behan's *The Quare Fellow*, directed by Cathy Burke. Her assistant later worked assisting at the Trafalgar Studio and she phoned me and another cast member to ask if we wanted to understudy a play called *Shoot the Crow*. It was set in Belfast and was about bathroom tilers. I was iffy but was told I would be covering Jim Norton and the other cover was a hilarious bould buck, Rooney from Co. Armagh, covering Jimmy Nesbit. After an understudy rehearsal on stage the actors arrived for the show and we went onto the roof, wide and flat, to do lines. We were a third of the way through when a stage manager hurtled up and said to us 'leave now'. We had been sitting around what we discovered was a huge round ventilation shaft above the stage. The cast were hearing a ghostly repetition of their play about two pages ahead of their performance. The humiliation.

Oengus MacNamara

I always feel an overwhelming sense of duty when I approach the stage door. None more so than the Trafalgar Theatre's, when I was doing *The Grinning Man*.

I think that's what stage doors mean to me, a symbol that represents the responsibility to deliver the best show I could possibly give. Stepping across that threshold as a company member is a privileged position to be in, and one in which I will never take for granted or abuse. For there is no better feeling, after a successful show, than confronting the world outside knowing that you have justified your existence for being behind the stage door!

Louis Maskell

Trafalgar Theatre

Dante wrote of the entrance to hell: 'Abandon Hope, all ye who enter here.' But at the stage door: 'Accept the gift of hope, all ye who enter here!'

It was such a privilege to be welcomed through the stage door at the Drury Lane. There was a theatre on that site a hundred years before the American Revolution. Imagine!! More than at any other theatre, I felt connected to the long line of players before me – all the glorious 'rogues and vagabonds' who, like me, made London their home.

Every time I went in the door at the Palace Theatre and read 'The world's greatest artistes have passed and will pass through these doors', I felt proud but also a bit of a fraud. I was not 'great' – I was just blessed to be 'good enough' to be allowed entrance. My dream had come true. That little girl from Kansas had grown up to be an 'artiste'!

Valda Aviks

Me and Bette Davis.

In 1975 Bette Davis appeared at the London Palladium, showing clips from her films and answering questions from the audience. How brave.

The first question was, 'Is your hair your own?' Next question!

'If they were to make a film of your life story, who would you like to play you? I suggest Marty Feldman.'

'Who's Marty Feldman?' came the cold reply.

The guy next to me offered me his binoculars, saying, 'Here, have a look. You can see all the wrinkles.'

Fed up with all this dissing of that great actress, I took round a note, at the interval, to the stage door – 'Ms Davis, I am a poor acting student, but would very much like to take you to dinner. I'll come to the stage door after the performance.'

So, my first experience of a West End stage door was waiting to take a legendary Hollywood actress to dinner.

I waited. And waited. And waited…

Eventually, I had to go get my last bus home.

Garry Cooper

The London Palladium

Stage Door means so many things to me. Anonymously walking through that door like so many artists before and after you. It's that entrance to your second home, the beginning of a daily ritual. There is always an energy about the place, the anticipation of what's about to come. To be greeted by a stage door keeper who is a massive part of that extended theatre family and always a friend, your first and last port of call. It always hits me how special Stage Door is when friends and family come to visit and are being signed in; it's a different world to them and there's always an air of excitement about it. Leaving through Stage Door to be greeted by so many people who want to say hi afterwards, to hear their stories and how the show has had an effect on them. The selfies, the chats and the post-show buzz on the other side of that door is what I miss most.

Mark Dugdale

There's nothing more comforting than arriving at a theatre where the stage door keeper welcomes you with open arms.

Most stage door keepers are great; however, I hold lovely memories of some exceptional ones. I remember I once lost a ring in my dressing room and everyone came outside the stage door, routing through the rubbish bins looking for it. It wasn't found but the sense of camaraderie was terrific!

Stage door keepers are always there for you, go the extra mile and always with a smile!

Lyn Paul

The Phoenix Theatre

I didn't feel remotely worthy when I was given the title – my first paid job in theatre. It was loaded with mythology, mysticism and too much importance. 'Stage Door Keeper.' Keeper. The keeper of the door through which artists enter carrying their plays to present and performances to give and music to play. Clocks have keepers, and lochs, and lighthouses. They keep time ticking, water flowing, they guard the light. I wasn't sure what I was a guardian of, but I knew I was the first person visitors saw on arrival and the last when they left. I had keys that opened every door in the building, waking the theatre up and closing it down at night. I listened alone to the shows over the speakers late into the evenings. It was impossibly romantic – to me, anyway. Whatever it was I was 'keeping', I was so proud to join the long list of people doing it, past, present and future.

James Graham

After spending many years passing through a number of stage doors it becomes your everyday norm and your door of work. The magic of a stage door only becomes very apparent when a 'muggle' stumbles across them, getting lost on London's busy streets. A small insignificant door to the side of a building. They see the sign and quickly become very excited, asking around to have their photo taken. I take great pleasure in interrupting these photo shoots to enter Stage Door. See the shock and awe on their faces when I pass, hearing them whisper, 'I wonder what they do? Do you think they are an actor?'

These moments remind me how lucky I am to be part of a secret, mystical team that creates magic on stage. Through creativity, teamwork, spotlights, sequins, and maybe some grease paint, thespians have the ability to create wonder on stage. That my everyday normal is an exciting different world to another and that I am very fortunate to be a part of it.

Emma Sheppard

STAGE
DOOR

STATIONE

TOWER
COURT WC2

St. Martin's Theatre

The West End stage door has always been a special place for me. My first show in the West End was at the Ambassadors; its stage door is down a little side street (Tower Court), which also houses the stage door for *The Mousetrap*. I remember on hot afternoons sitting outside, chatting to the cast from that show. Feeling part of a community and part of a history. The glamour of the West End to a kid from an immigrant, totally non-theatrical, family in Croydon was something that I was now part of. It felt exciting and it felt like an honour. I especially love that most stage doors are down little side streets and are often cramped and tatty. That certainly adds to the glamour. My favourite coffee and pastry shop in Soho is Maison Bertaux – it's arty and shabby-chic but with delicious food and coffee. That's exactly what West End stage doors are like. Like a throwback to the 50s, but with style and content and beautiful, vibrant clientele.

Paul Bazely

It's really difficult to write anything about the stage door at the Ambassadors Theatre. Don't get me wrong – it's not that it didn't fill me with excitement to pass through it every day for twelve weeks, or that the wave of nostalgia and loss I feel every time I've walked by it since, no longer allowed to venture inside, isn't completely overwhelming. It's more that, for me: this door is the lid on a box full of wonderful memories. Write about the door itself? Maybe you're squeezing 100 words out of me, at best. Write about what happens as soon as you open the door? Now we're cooking…

Perhaps I could reminisce about watching December storms from our dressing room window as I listen to the audience filter in. Or possibly I could write about keeping my regular clothes on underneath my costume on Saturday matinées, so as to optimise the time it took me to get changed after the show, buying myself a marginally longer swim at the Oasis, or being able to catch a 4 o'clock film at the Odeon Covent Garden. Instead, I've chosen to write about absolutely demolishing my colleagues in a three-month-long Shut the Box tournament.

For the uninitiated, Shut the Box is a game where a few dice rolls dictate your score for that day. Sure, I could bore you with details of the daily back-and-forth, the roll disputes and the lucky streaks. Or preferably, I could just let you, dear reader, know that in the three-way finale on the 4th of January 2020, I managed to whoop every single one of my opponents and walk home with a stone-cold wad of cash poking out my denims. Believe you me, there is no finer feeling than prying some Lizzies out of Simon Lipkin's grip whilst he tries to barter with you ('Would you take vouchers?', 'I need these to pay off the mob', etc. Gimme a break).

Every morning since, I've woken up full of immense joy knowing that I will forever be the Ambassadors Theatre's greatest Shut the Box player, and that thick wooden stage door will be a permanent reminder of that for as long as it's standing. Pop that in your pipe and smoke it.

Preston Nyman

A stage door is an entrance to another home. I enter anonymously and climb the stairs to my little heaven. A refuge where I become something I am not, but I am still myself. Behind this door is a loud family gathering full of laughter, tears, comfort, joy, creativity, sweat, support and most of all love. Egos? There is always one, but they are just fragile and can soften in the right light. I exit as I came, and walk off into the darkness of the night. The stage door is the entrance to my home away from home.

The stage door has changed from when I started in the business. It's an after-show now, with security and barriers and people wanting selfies. I miss the stage door where I could just slip away quietly into the night.

Lauren Ward

The Ambassadors Theatre

The stage door is where theatre meets the everyday world. The place where you find yourself lingering around; whether it be soaking up your daily intake of vitamin D before returning to a pitch-black theatre, thinking about the day's rehearsals or just chatting to a passing friend. The stage door brings people together, people you already know, people you'd like to know, or even your theatrical idol. It's a place where you can bond with friends and colleagues. A place where you can find yourself happy, sad, overwhelmed or pumped with adrenaline. The stage door welcomes you and waves you goodbye as you start or end a production. Each time you find that new stage door it's like finding a portal into another world.

Jessica Hung Han Yun

I still feel the way I did at nine years old when I walked up to my first stage door. It still feels special every time.

You know walking in you are a part of something spectacular and that you are about to not only do what you love, but you get to bring joy to the audiences. You get to transport people everywhere, taking them away from reality for a few hours.

Coffee in hand, bare-faced, ready to go into your little safe space. It never ever gets old.

You meet new people at stage doors. People who love the show. People who love theatre.
For these people they get to see you after the performance they have just seen and get a glimpse of who really played that role. It is special to them and it is incredibly special to me.

Natalie McQueen

One of my favourite pastimes working in these amazing buildings is the awkward squeeze past guests who are waiting to see other cast members as you leave the stage door. Due to the age of many of the theatres the space just inside a stage door entrance is tiny. I'll never forget smacking a certain movie star flush across the face with my rucksack as I ran to get my train. 'I'm so sorry,' I said to her. She simply replied with 'That's OK, well done.' I still missed the train.

Gavin Spokes

The Savoy Theatre

Stage Door
Open Door
To
The Beginning
The Work
The Character
The Rehearsal
The Show
Opening Night, Last Night
The Precious People who greet you with
Your Post, Your Key, Your Room Number,
They Know
They've Seen Us
Come and Go
Linda, Cathy, Sandra
Ned, Vincent Sarah.
STAY EXACTLY WHERE YOU ARE

WE'RE COMING BACK

Niamh Cusack

Stage Door has always meant a lot to me. It's the first moment when you engage with the evening's work. The interactions with the public can happen here and send you on your way with an encouraging compliment or two. Stage door keepers are usually the best informed about the goings-on in the building, too, so you get your gossip and an early warning if something's amiss that performance. At the end of the night, there's also the satisfying 'clocking off' feeling, like a momentary decompression chamber, before you step into the real world, again.

Paterson Joseph

The Aldwych Theatre

To us designers, the stage doors mean something slightly different than, let's say, to performers. The theatre doesn't become a home to us for a long period but just a short while – our time there is brief and intense. So when I think about the stage door I am thinking of the time during technical rehearsals: the set has just been built – costumes are starting to come together and it is the first time since I designed the show back in my studio all those months ago that I get to see everything together again. This is exhilarating and terrifying in equal measures – will it all come together the way I had envisaged it?

We designers are one of the first people to arrive in the building in the morning and one of the last to leave late at night. The minute we enter we are being swallowed by the building: all the different departments who create aspects of our design – each worker needing our attention, our comment, our advice, our approval. We attend every minute of the rehearsal and as soon as the break starts we are being pulled in all directions to answer the questions we were not available for whilst sitting in the auditorium. So when approaching the stage door in the morning I always run everything through in my head. I mentally prepare myself and brace myself for the day. I take a last deep breath just outside the door – I take in the last bit of daylight that I will probably get to see for the rest of the day and I enter: stepping across this threshold between the natural world outside and this imaginary world we are building in this crazy and all-consuming way.

The strange thing is – just a few days after press night – when we designers are done with our work and move on to the next show – the stage door is instantly a bit of a stranger again. It's not like walking into your own house anymore – it's like walking into the house of a very close friend. It's so incredibly familiar, but at the same time you don't fully belong any more – it is now the house of the cast and the show crew alone.

Anna Fleischle

One of my most meaningful stage door experiences was one of my first.

I had come to performing late. Being physically disabled, I didn't realise it would even be a possibility to fulfil my childhood dreams of being an actor. But by my mid-twenties, I went for it, and one of my first productions was leading a dance theatre show. The cast was made up of the most extraordinary able-bodied contemporary dancers, and I was the only actor and the only disabled performer. At the stage door after opening night, a nine-year-old boy was giddy to meet me and told me with deep sincerity that he wanted to be like me when he grew up. I was deeply moved, and honestly shocked – I was still living in a world where disability was seen as lesser and disabled people were to be pitied, and here was this able-bodied kid who singled out myself, amongst a cast of the most physically dexterous and impressive able-bodied dancers, as who he aspired to be like. This kid's words felt like the confirmation that I truly was living the dreams I had abandoned when I had my spinal cord injury, and I was doing the kid inside me proud. It also further proved to me that disabled bodies being seen and celebrated on stages not only helped disabled people like me but also shifted the perception of who disabled people are for the abled majority. That we could be heroes kids look up to, not just victims adults look down on. My dad's morbid response to this was 'I hope he doesn't do anything to his spine.' I hope so too, haha, but even if, God forbid, something were to happen to his spine, I know he could still be someone's hero.

Daniel Monks

The Donmar Warehouse

There is a very particular kind of romance about a stage door. A portal between worlds. Their humble, hidden locations, usually in alleyways or side streets, cleverly disguising their magical properties. They are the liminal threshold through which no traveller returns unchanged. If you doubt their sacred nature, try leaving through one as a performer with the story still being told, and the blasphemy hits you like the most potent of taboo.

Michael Sheen

I don't get the notion that actors should walk into a theatre by the same entrance as audiences. I never have.

The stage door for me is a portal between this life, these streets, that fish and chip wrapper scuffing about the road on a bleak-looking Monday… and the world of the play.

Like shadows, and often as grey as the day, we push our way into some dark passageway and disappear… and then all feathered and shiny and utterly transformed… there we are on the other side, in another life, being someone else. Telling our story.

It's magical, and we acting tribe must have mystery. The stage door is the stuff of dreams.

Lia Williams

STAGE DOOR

The Harold Pinter Theatre

The first time I spent any real time outside a stage door was at the Albery Theatre in 1986. It has since been renamed the Noël Coward, but when I was 19 and auditioning for a chorus line it was still the Albery – named after Sir Bronson Albery, who had presided as its manager for a great many years. I had seen the film of a chorus line, so when they advertised in *The Stage* newspaper that they were casting for a UK touring version, I knew I wanted it. It was a cattle call. Something we call an 'open audition'. Hundreds of performers turn up all day hoping to be seen, and as I didn't have an agent, I decided to get on the train to London and try my luck. I had always been told you made your own luck, so with that in mind, I left home early so I could beat the crowds I knew would be there.

It was my first London audition, which was scheduled to start at 10am. I wanted the job so much I got there at 7am. I will never forget walking up to the stage door and realising I was the first one there. I ended up being number 1 out of 1700 performers who showed up to audition that day. I had to return through that stage door five more times as they whittled us down to the final cast. Each time I walked through that door the show became more and more real. I remember on the last day there were about 20 of us in line under the stage door sign and it slowly dawned on me, as I asked each person which of the parts they were there for, that no one else was up for Maggie. I was the only one. Could it mean the job was mine? We were then all asked to stand on stage, and it was there that we were told we had been given the part. We all literally jumped for joy and I spent the next hour outside the Albery Theatre stage door swapping telephone numbers and hugging my future castmates.

Every time I pass that stage door it reminds me that dreams come true. That if you want something you can always have it. You just have to want it enough.

Ruthie Henshall

What a special place this is to me. The memories made walking through this door for a year and a half were unbelievable. In 2006 at 20 years old I landed my first leading role in the original cast of *Avenue Q*. The show was the first in the newly named Noël Coward Theatre (previously the Albery). Newly decorated dressing rooms… how was I to know every room after that wouldn't come with a chaise and an en suite. Me being me I added a Nintendo Wii, because, ya know… class… I remember one day they were holding an open day to show off the new look and there was a knock at the door… 'come in', I said. By the way, I was topless and playing said Wii (my room, my rules); the door opens and Alan Rickman enters. I obviously panic, I'm 20 and a big *Die Hard* fan. He looks around. 'Very nice,' he says. 'Wanna play?' I say. 'No thanks,' he said and quietly left the room. And I thought… I guess this is showbiz.

The alleyway that connects the stage doors of the Noël Coward and Wyndham's was our playground. Chatting through cup phones from window to window between theatres with whatever company was performing opposite (Derek Jacobi never answered), coming out for a game of badminton (complete with net), seeing the History Boys smoking outside like naughty school kids behind the bike sheds, all the way down to sparklers outside on bonfire night. It was joyous. The amazing generous wonderful people who would wait to say hello outside after a show. The brilliant faces that worked in those two theatres (and the bar opposite) that you'd see every day. The truth is… more than any other theatre I've performed in in the West End… it was home. It's where I learned what my life would be like. What working meant. Making mistakes. Making friends. I didn't know what was ahead of me the first time I walked through that door. I was scared and nervous and I had no idea if I could do it… the thing I've learned is… you always feel like that every time you walk through a new one of these doors. But every time you step underneath that magical sign… STAGE DOOR… you remember how God damn lucky you are… but hey… you always remember your first… here's to the memories.

Simon Lipkin

The Noël Coward Theatre

When I started, it was all about the Royal Court. And one constant throughout was John, who worked on the stage door. Before an audition, I would sit right next to his desk, waiting to be called upstairs. Sometimes I was relaxed and chatty, other times less so. He was very good at judging where I was at and I was grateful. I began to work there and I'd see him most days; we celebrated press nights together and we got to know each other. Over the years, I'd stay behind after auditions to catch up. He left soon after a bereavement, having worked there my whole career. I think of John often. I hope he's doing well.

Tom Brooke

Stage doors are portals from the outside world to the inner sanctums of theatres. I gazed at them for years wondering how to cross the threshold.
Would I belong?
Who chooses who is allowed in?

Some years later I stood in the number-one dressing room, overlooking the stage door, at the Royal Court theatre. I was told it was where George Devine and Laurence Olivier were based, because they had a view down to the alley, to see who was waiting at the stage door.

I was a new artistic director, and gave some thought to the 'event' of entering the building; how we managed where actors were put, waiting for auditions, and how our stage door staff were supported in best holding that threshold.

I soon realised that so many of the key conversations were happening just outside the stage door. Writers in their previews, talking to their directors; young people, attending workshops, lingering for one more piece of advice, as well as actors laughing with the stage crew, sharing roll-ups.

The last thing to happen in the rhythm of a theatre's day is the light of the stage door going out, the ghosts of all the conversations and minglings through that day still present, the threshold space of dreams.

Ian Rickson

STAGE
DOOR

The Royal Court Theatre

The first time I ever tried to find the stage door of The Theatre Royal Haymarket, it took me ten minutes. The second time it took me twenty. Readers of *Harry Potter and the Order of the Phoenix* will be familiar with the magic that keeps 12 Grimmauld Place a mystery to outsiders, and I can only assume it's the same flavour of abracadabra that has been applied to 19 Suffolk Street.

TRH's stage door exists in one of those slices of London that is apparitive. The moment one strides with purpose toward it, the fabric of space-time tears, subsuming modernity and forcing the inadvertent time-traveller to check one's path for horse-drawn carriages and choleric chimney sweeps. London as imagined by Dickens, by Woodhouse, by Americans.

And at the back left of this tarmacked paradox, another tool for teleportation – though one that teleports the folk who've entered the building via the front.

I have arrived at work through that door, I have left for home through that door – but I have never done either without awe or a sense that, within the reaches of its doorstep hex, the world becomes something else. Mind you, that could just be the effect of what they smoke in the doorkeeper's office.

Rufus Hound

As a child, I remember waiting at the stage door of the Royal Ballet for Darcey Bussell to sign my programme. Through that little girl's eyes, I glimpsed a secret world of impossible glamour, foreign and unknowable. Years later and instead of waiting, I am now walking through that magical portal; the keeper of the kingdom is smiling and waving me through. A kettle boils. The door closes. The atmosphere is thick with history and laced with the sweat, tears and emotion of those who came before me. In my dressing room, I take a seat. My reflection in the mirror stares back at me, my heart thumps, a tiny mouse scurries past. Again, I wait.

Zoë Tapper

The Theatre Royal Haymarket

Stage Doors Personified

Stage doors are both your passive observer and your active protector.
They've been a witness to the comings and goings throughout the entirety of theatre history.
(Oh, the stories they could tell!)
They coolly watch people sign in and out of their daily working lives.
Watch a person start the evening with anxiety and nerves and end it with a sigh of relief, a smile of satisfaction (one hopes).
'Survived another one.'
They witness successes and failures.
They witness the mundanity of the daily slog.
They witness humanity at their best, worst and everything in between.
They witness the banter, the rudeness, the kindness, the heartache, the unspoken understandings.
They watch flowers and press night cards come and go.
They've seen it all.

However, do not be fooled by their apparent indifference. Stage doors are in fact the gatekeepers of 'Backstage-Ville'. Privy to a certain few.
Inexplicably alluring.
(On a personal note: a small subconscious part of me still expects to be rugby tackled to the ground every time I turn up to work – 'Oi, you! You're trespassing!' 'There's been an error.' 'Sorry, who are you?' 'How dare I/you presume I/you have a right to access theatre's most inner sanctum?' 'Out! Get out!' – Y'know, the classic imposter syndrome yak-yak-yakking away.)
And yet.
An exhalation as I leave the Outside World at my back.
Stage doors become a sanctuary from The Noise.
Stage doors are excellent at keeping those pesky, unnecessary thoughts at bay.
The moment you step over that threshold, you are no longer thinking about bills, unanswered emails, neglected chores, that weekly shop, blah blah blah.
There's now room for silence.
Focus.
Actual brain space to get on with the job.
Stage doors stand guard, protect, give permission and allow what one needs to do without guilt.

Patsy Ferran

The stage door is the point of no return! The first preview arrives, and once you've stepped over that threshold, all there is ahead of you is the show; the thing you've spent weeks rehearsing and which tonight finally gets its unveiling. All the nerves of that first night and every night after that are in every stage door. These totally inconspicuous (and almost always weathered!) doors, with their lonely light shining out onto whichever unassuming back street that they lead out onto, are an entrance into the unknown – and all the more exciting for it!!

Joshua McGuire

The Dominion Theatre

The Piccadilly Theatre

The first port of call when we arrive,
That friendly face,
Keeper of the Keys to our temporary second home.

Stopping for a quick 'How you doing?' chat, and nearly missing the warm-up call. 'So and so called', 'You've got a parcel', 'You putting a pound in for the Lotto?'

Sophie at The Piccadilly has baked some delicious cupcakes for charity, and has shared a website, so I now own a fantastic pair of deep purple flared cord trousers.
I've been yearning for curried goat, and Jamie's made some and slides it over the counter.
Noel at The Hackney Empire has always got your back, and a welcoming hug.
Linda at The National, wonderful lady, over 40 years, the stories she could tell. When she retires she should write a bestseller.

The industry turning out to honour the dapper legend that is 'Uncle Harry', celebrating '40 Happy Years' at The Shaftesbury, is a testimony to the importance of our stage door and the tone that they can set for the building.

Some departments may not cross paths at all, but Stage Door sees and knows everyone. Great stage door keepers are worth their weight in gold.

Sharon D Clarke

'You must be EXHAUSTED!'
'And today you've done two?'
'I loved the sets. I loved her.'
'And how was it for you?'

'How do you remember all those words?'
'The costumes must be fun!'
'So glad I caught it. Just in time!'
'It's not for me. It's for my son.'

'You got changed so quickly!'
'It's gonna be a smash.'
'Wasn't he in that thing?'
'Quick drink then I'll dash.'

Mark Gatiss

Stage doors often come with an innate sense of elitism.

An insinuation that those lucky enough to be allowed through them have a capacity to do something that those on the outside don't. It's a funny divide, considering we all end up in the same room eventually. Separated by nothing other than some lights and the edge of a stage. Yet the illusion of separation is immense. A sense that on the other side of that stage lies a portal to another world. A heightened level of emotion. Predicaments that we are riveted by yet hope to never have the misfortune of living through ourselves. Unless it's a romance... We all hope to have the misfortune of living through a few of those.

I have come to find that this sense of elitism, the elitism that appears to be behind the stage door or past the edge of that stage, the idea that theatre is for the culturally adept, the socially superior or the economically blessed, is nothing more than an illusion. It's just as much of an illusion as the faraway world depicted on stage.

As an outsider to all things theatrical, I've found that stage door to be a portal into the only place a misfit like myself can feel at home. A place where an odd person's idiosyncrasies are championed instead of suppressed and a place where thinking differently is the only real valid currency.

Taz Skylar

Her Majesty's Theatre

One of my most memorable stage door moments was at the Cambridge Theatre on a warm summer's evening after a particularly wonderful show of *Matilda*. I walked out to be greeted by a few groups of people who had watched the show, loved it and kindly took the time to stay behind to tell us so. I had a sudden vivid flashback of being a student and standing at that very same stage door many years ago, envying the lives of the exiting performers and dreaming about what it might really be like to be living that life. As I walked to the station that night to get my train I grinned from ear to ear thinking: 'I've done it! I'm doing it!' The young me simply wouldn't believe her luck.

Marianne Benedict

If I could perfect the art of writing and talking about theatres without sounding like an awful pseud, I'd either have reached some kind of professional nirvana or I'd cease to exist, because try as I might, it's nigh on impossible.

I want to say that there's nothing magical about stage doors. That they're JUST DOORS. They're the BACK door, for goodness' sake. The goods entrance. They're usually a bit grubby, annoyingly hard to find, awkward to navigate, and next to some kind of invisible door-urinal. But, irritatingly for the sake of my mission to not sound cosmic, they actually are – oh no, here it comes – they're some kind of mystical portal. OK, phew, I've got that out of my system. They're not, of course.

Something does happen, though, when you go into a theatre through the stage door. Most of the crap you've carried around with you all day stays outside, and suddenly a whole different, creative, timeless crap is yours to embrace. They're the place where you arrive to work at, let's face it, a ludicrous time to start work, and where you sign out, more awake and adrenalised than anyone should be at 10.30pm. Where a smattering of people stands to take a selfie or get something signed. A selfie with me? No no, of course not; they're here for Ralph Fiennes, to whom I'll make sure to say goodnight, so people know that I'm (a) cool and (b) also in the play with Ralph Fiennes.

They're where some outrageously popular people collect cards and gifts they've been sent by well-wishers, and where I occasionally collect something I've ordered online and had delivered to the theatre in case nobody's at home to sign for it. They feel like they haven't changed since the theatre was built in whatever year all the theatres were built. The people who work at Stage Door are almost invariably absolutely excellent and have better theatrical anecdotes than I will ever be able to recount in the pub. They also generally know – and this is the point, so forgive me – how much it means to an actor to go through the stage door and somehow at once arrive at work and come home.

Ferdinand Kingsley

The Cambridge Theatre

Stage doors have always held a sense of excitement for me. They are the portal between the real world and the adventure in our invented reality and the romance of the theatre itself. It's a right of passage for those of us who had fallen in love with going to the theatre and aspired to work in it, to be finally being allowed into the secret backstage world and becoming part of the industry. Each stage door has its own character, guarded by keepers who invest them with a little of their own personality. They always give me a sense of coming home and being part of a company. Once the stage door keeper knows your name, and you theirs, it's like being part of the building and the history of the place. There is always a thrill crossing from real life into the lives and realities we create on stage. I always feel pride and a little bit special when I'm allowed through them.

Lez Brotherston

So, stage door! Stage door to me means, you know, it's the kind like the door to Narnia, you have your normal life, and then you have show call, you get up you work out you have lunch with a friend, and then you go through that door, and you go into a world that is not like going through any other door to any other job… it's a world where we all live in the dark, and each night we create something magical – an experience, a story, escapism. Going through that door allows me to go and do my favourite job in the world. It's also a portal to a breath of fresh air and a glimpse of daylight during tech, and a breather and maybe an ice cream at the interval! Those West End venues get HOT in the summertime!

And then coming out of that door is a whole different ball game! So, coming out, you often see crowds of people greeting the actors, congratulating them – if you have a child cast there are hoards of friends and family greeting the kids, and it's always so joyous, because it's always people laughing, smiling, having had a wonderful evening and congratulating the people that made that happen. And it's wonderful.

And then sometimes you work on shows with really famous people… and then it's a bit different! I worked on a show a couple of years ago with a famous Hollywood actor. And for three months, at the end of each evening, I would approach that stage door from the inside. And I would push it open, and every night I would hear this huge hopeful gasp… which would then immediately turn into a huge disappointed groan when they realised… that I was just me…

And then one night when I was leaving, to get out the door I found myself stepping over half of the Fellowship of the Ring. The One Ring – from *The Lord of the Rings*. Casually obscuring my way was Ian McKellen, Orlando Bloom and Adam Brown – Gandalf, Legolas and Ori – sat in my way, shuffling aside to let me through to catch the next 319 to Streatham…

Tamsin Withers

The Vaudeville Theatre

The stage door of the Garrick Theatre is a unique place. Entering through the outer door on Charing Cross Road, an alleyway takes you round to a small courtyard. From there a door to your right leads you into the circle of the auditorium, one up steps to your left to the warren of dressing rooms. Which way to go? There aren't many occasions, perhaps only in a downpour, when you don't linger in the courtyard itself for a moment before deciding. It's a crossroads: real life back down the alley; your night's work over the threshold to the right and all the nerves, throat sweets and human accomplices in the dressing rooms to your left. But of course, many of those accomplices are lingering like you, and will gladly delay your choice. People smoke, chat, eat, take and give notes, scratch chins, meet family and friends post-show, make phone calls, etc.: an alfresco stage door-osteria-office-green room in one. From there, in fact, one can even be reminded that yours isn't the only show in town; the dressing rooms of the Duke of York's next door overlook this busy cloister – same nerves, different sweets, old friends. During my stays at the Garrick the courtyard has been kept in full bloom and good order by the redoubtable Sylvia and Jo; gatekeepers, counsellors, ravens.

Stage doors are places for crossing over – at the Garrick Theatre, this can take a while and is much the better for it.

Hadley Fraser

It's a pre-show ritual we all go through, the first point of call. I guess the show begins the moment we step through those doors. Always greeted with a smile. See you again in three hours. Show done. The ritual ends. I miss it.

Karl Queensborough

The Garrick Theatre

The stage door. Gateway to the magic? Mysterious portal to a world of dreams? Most theatre lovers have a romantic idea of these modest and, more often than not, shabby entrances (a reminder of the days when actors were regarded as lesser mortals and had to use what was regarded as effectively a tradesmen's entrance.) My heart still beats a little faster with anticipation when I enter a stage door – despite its usually unglamorous not to say frequently grubby aspect.

Stage door keepers fulfil a vital function, and not only as protectors but passers-on of messages, gifts, and some become friends. They become part of your life – particularly if you are on a long run. At the Royal National Theatre, many years earlier on the South Bank – the stage door ushered you into what always reminded me as a hotel lobby. In fact, the famous backstage bar was only up the next flight of stairs and many a staggering drunken actor would greet those of us performing that night, trying to negotiate the steps having had a few too many tipples after rehearsal, hoping to meander home. I remember catching the late great Tony Haygarth as he stumbled down the last step, convivial but roaring drunk, and helping him out of the building prior to my nearly four hours in and out of costume as part of an enormous ensemble of Ibsen's *Peer Gynt* that night.

Many years later I was at St. Martin's where *The Mousetrap* was still running and I was treading in the footsteps of legions of actors playing the role of Paravicini. Being there for almost a year, we, as the cast, inhabited the Tower Court alleyway in all weathers – drinking coffee in the sun on matinee days, chatting to actor friends using the alley as a shortcut to the Actors Centre and the Tristan Bates while we hovered in the doorway in costume. And chatting at the stage door now manned by Pat, who would listen to mainstream jazz on his portable vinyl player. Somehow the place seemed less grubby.

Later I was at The Old Vic on the other side of the river just seven years ago. The profession had changed. In the cast, we had an international film star, Richard Armitage, so there were always queues of fans lining up outside the stage door. The play was sold out from the first preview to the last night, and there was definitely a smell of success in the air. Yaël Farber's production of *The Crucible* had attracted a lot of interest and critical acclaim and the stage door was continually a hub of excitement and activity. The atmosphere was always quite electric outside this particular stage door, and I have fond memories of the stage door keeper Ned, who always used to summon us from our dressing room with a tannoy announcement when passing on a first night card or bouquet: 'Will Neil Salvage come to the stage door, where he will receive something to his advantage?'

And now, the stage doors are closed, the theatres are empty husks and we look back with gratitude at an era of excitement and creativity, encapsulated by the bustle outside these portals and yearning for them to open again. Let us hope it will be soon.

Neil Salvage

The Lyceum Theatre

I must have taken about a hundred pictures of the recently refurbished and renamed Sondheim Theatre stage door, formerly the Queen's, of course! I would walk into work every day, bagel in hand, juggling my skinny cap, stand in the middle of the road and quickly scramble to pull my phone out of my pocket to take yet another picture of it. My camera roll got very repetitive. This stage door signified the end of a really long wait. I first stepped onto a West End stage when I was 17 (totally inexperienced, untrained and terrified) auditioning for *Les Misérables*. It wasn't until 11 years later I made my West End debut, in that very show. Every single time I would approach the stage door to start work I just couldn't quite believe I was finally there… so I couldn't resist documenting it with 'Oh, but just one more photo!'

Jessie Hart

As someone who has wanted to be a performer for as long as I can remember, I always imagined the first time I walked through a West End stage door would be one of those momentous and memorable occasions. As it turned out, my first would be for an audition (funnily enough at the Queen's – now the Sondheim – where I was to eventually get my first job). Sick with nerves, I didn't really stop to take it all in! Equally, the first time we entered the Sondheim as a new cast it was all so much of a whirlwind I don't have a memory of the stage door 'moment'. But in the months that followed often I'd just step out into the street after a rehearsal, or between shows, to grab some food or pop to the shops. Hair in pin curls, no makeup, people passing by without a second glance. Stepping out into the daylight on an ordinary weekday, often into the rain, with the real world continuing to bustle on, just how I left it. And it's in these extremely unglamorous and mundane instants that I'd have my little 'moments'. People passing in the street have absolutely no idea what magic is being created just behind that very unassuming door. And I get to pass through this portal in and out of these different worlds at my leisure. How lucky am I?!

Kathy Peacock

The Sondheim Theatre

The stage door for me is the main entrance in and out of the theatre. It has a familiarity far greater than any of the front of house areas. It's where the butterflies start on a day of technical rehearsals and where you finally breathe out and relax when leaving on opening night. It's the one place in the building all departments use, so it's also a great place to cross paths with people working on the show who you might not have seen for days of sitting tensely in the dark whilst they work away four floors above you. Often located down alleys or back streets, they have a power far greater than their often modest appearances, and I think that brings even the biggest egos down to earth – even if, in some cases, by only a tiny bit!

Howard Hudson

Glimpsing those two words, trigger an intake of breath.
A gateway stirring emotions, replenishing your heart with –
Happiness, nervousness, excitement, peace.
A reminder of the years of training, practice and hard work.
Crossing the threshold into another world,
Where everyone is on common ground.

Under the sign, after the curtain falls,
A conclusion of a theatrical experience.
Meet stars, newcomers, veterans and ones to watch.
Celebrate and congratulate from one side of a barrier,
Thank, appreciate and converse from the other.
Say goodnight, then leave one home for another.

Jonathan Andrew Hume

The Royal Opera House

There is a sacrosanct feeling to crossing through a stage door when you are employed at a theatre. I remember as a kid going to the theatre and seeing a stage door sign, it just felt amazing. 'What goes on through that doors? Who are these special people going in there?'

The thing about a stage door that is so gorgeous, is that you must earn the right to walk through it. Every detail of it is simply magical, being greeted by the stage door person, signing in, walking to your dressing room! As I type this I feel myself getting excited. The sense when you first arrive that you will never feel comfortable with these new surroundings and yet the palpable sense of sadness when you leave for the final time. Another chapter has come to an end. It is the very first and very last place you go on your job. It bookends it.

As actors, we spend so much of our careers living on hopes and dreams. There is something so reassuring about the soft glow of a stage door sign and the sense of reward when you walk in. You took the risk of this lifestyle, and you were lucky enough to get the part… this time. So here is your reward. For this short space of time, you can walk through this special doorway that 'civilians' can only marvel at. I adore it and truly cannot wait to be walking through one again. I love them all, but if I had to pick one that pips the others to the post… it would be the stage door of the Wyndham's Theatre. Absolute heaven.

Andy Nyman

Wyndham's Theatre

When I was in the original cast of *Harry Potter and the Cursed Child* at the Palace Theatre there would be a huge queue outside the stage door after every performance waiting to have their programmes signed. To give the queue some order, they placed barriers outside the stage door and around the corner of the building into Shaftesbury Avenue. As someone with a VERY minor role in the production, I was only once asked for my autograph, which led to a few others handing over their programmes with a look of 'I've no idea who you are or what you did in the show, but might as well get your signature since I'm here'. The rest of the time I'd exit the stage door to see expectant faces light up, only to almost as instantly fade to indifference when they didn't recognise me. After a few weeks of this, I took to leaving the building via a side door and so avoid the humiliation. It was during that same time that I became aware that one of my co-understudies who covered Dumbledore was consistently being mistaken for the actor who played the role. I don't think the principal actor was entirely happy about that!

Andrew McDonald

I love stage doors. I think the public and the audiences are fascinated by them too, and by the people who pass through them. Often I arrive or leave work to a crowd of people waiting by the stage door, hoping to meet their hero, to meet the actors they have just seen on stage that have moved them so much that they have had to come by the stage door to let them know. Even waiting to ask the crew about the secrets of the show.

For me, though, a stage door is made by its stage door keeper, the person behind the intercom, the person who lets you in, who is there to answer any questions, point you in the right direction, to take in your post and often there for a good chat. These people who often sit tucked away in a tiny corner are what make stage doors such a special place.

Claire Roberts

The Lyric Theatre

In 2002 I met my wife. At the time she was playing Sandy in *Grease* at the Victoria Palace Theatre in Victoria, London. I would meet her at the stage door sometimes, and we would often grab a post-show drink in the Stage Door Pub opposite the actual stage door of the VP. London buses would whizz by and the only place to get any food was actually in Victoria Station. Lots of happy memories for us both.

Fast forward to 2017, when I worked on *Hamilton* at the Victoria Palace Theatre in 2017/2018, the building itself was still undergoing a major amount of construction and refurbishments, so much so that the first performance of *Hamilton* in London was delayed. The stage door was literally like entering a building site, as many building materials would be delivered at the same time as our company and theatre staff (and builders) would pass through it. It was a crazy place of two worlds colliding – musical theatre and construction. That first year I was in *Hamilton* in London was exciting for lots of reasons, but witnessing the changes to the theatre and the stage door was very interesting and intense at times. With *Hamilton* came a huge fan base and that also meant somewhere was needed for some of the audiences to wait and say hi, get an autograph or get in the line for tickets, and that was next to a construction site at the Victoria Palace Theatre. Everyone involved in *Hamilton* in London for that first year, whether we were involved in the show or it was audiences, had to come to terms with an unfinished building.

Stage Door at the VP in 2002 and 2017 are two different worlds now. So much development has happened in that area, with lovely shops and restaurants to boot, now all a stone's throw from the VP stage door. When I was playing King George III in *Hamilton* my experience of that stage door was like no other. The juxtaposition between the hype and mania of the original London company of *Hamilton* and day to day major construction was a massive part of my experience in that building. Even though my time in *Hamilton* was a mixture of excitement, chaos and walking through that brand new stage door, one of my main memories will be greeting my future wife and feeling very much in love back in 2002!

Michael Jibson

'All the world's a stage,
And all the men and women merely players;
They have their exits and their entrances,
And one man (or woman) in their time plays many parts'

Lest we forget, we are all playing our individual roles in life. It's time for us to go back to playing ours.
Open Theatreland and turn our 'exeunt' into a 'manent'.

Jason Pennycooke

When I think of the stage door at a theatre, the first thing that comes to my mind and heart is 'magical'. So many people walk through those doors, from staff and performers to the semi-circle of the audience and fans of the show/cast that wait outside anxiously optimistic to meet them and get their signed programmes.

A favourite memory of mine was walking through the Victoria Palace Theatre for the first time as part of the original cast of *Hamilton*, having our first induction of the building. Being greeted by the wonderful staff and being shown to the stage to see the set for the first time was exhilarating. The stage door was like walking into what was going to be my second home. When the shows were up and running the incredible feeling of walking out of the stage door to the amazing fans who had nothing but love for the cast and show itself never got old.

The stage door is a saviour to so many of us, including myself, and I am sure that they will be busy once again with even more magical energy than before.

Christopher Tendai

The Victoria Palace Theatre

STAGE DOOR

It was press night for *Waitress* at the Adelphi and I'd been lent a gorgeous dress for the party. Unfortunately, as I was getting ready, the zip on my dress broke and wouldn't stay up (maybe I ate one too many pies)! I tried everything I could to fix it but had no luck, so headed downstairs to Stage Door for help.

The amazing woman on the stage door and her amazing friend from FOH dropped everything and did everything in their power to fix it. They eventually decided the best idea would be to safety-pin me in the dress, which was hilarious but completely worked! So off I headed to press night rocking safety pins all down the side of my outfit!

This is one of my favourite memories from that job and from a West End stage door. They really saved me that night, and I felt such unity and friendship at that moment. I then continued to feel that throughout my time at the Adelphi, and I will always be grateful for their kindness, good humour and welcoming warmth.

Laura Baldwin

Stage Door is the portal to the world of make-believe. It's always a pleasure to come out to the stage door after a show and find audience members waiting, beaming with excitement about what they have just watched. Many just want a picture to remember the occasion or signatures in the programme. But there are those who want to share with you what they have experienced and how the performances have touched them. I really enjoy listening to them retell their stories. How they laughed, cried and danced until the last cast member left the stage and the curtain came down. Often many are so moved by what they have seen, making correlations between the story, a character, a song and how it mirrors a personal moment in their own lives. The stage door experience is such a small moment in time, a meeting of minds and then it's over. Tomorrow we do all over again, same time, same place, new faces, more stories.

Matt Henry

Every stage door is an entrance to another world, a world you have created with a group of like-minded people, and every time you enter you leave your domestic life behind and escape from reality... well, sort of! Because now your reality is that magical space beyond... the theatre. Every stage door is blessed with a stage door keeper – your friend – your confidant – who keeps you in touch with the real world outside. No stage door is complete without them, and the moment they welcome you with your dressing room key, your post, and you greet your fellow actors, you feel that surge of adrenaline, and your new world can begin. Except none of us knows how long our new world will last – a season – a short run – a smash hit or a critical disaster, but, for now, it's your home...

Robert Lindsay

The Adelphi Theatre

I'm new to writing, so my timid ideas tend to hover around what I'm familiar with. One story focused on the inner workings of a run-down theatre, and the character which leaped to my mind most immediately was an omniscient stage door manager.

I had met people like him many times: magical, kind and wise; cut from the same stone as the first bricks laid; framed in their cocoons by posters and flowers; photos on a board suggesting a mastery of time itself ('That couldn't possibly be them with Greta Garbo, can it?'); old leather books (of spells?) and some strange-smelling elixir cooking on an open fire.

They look up. They greet you by name. ('How do they know my name?') Give a wink suggesting they know where you buried the body (but won't tell). Sometimes you have to answer a riddle, sometimes not. Then they hand you a key. Cast iron, in the best cases. You take it and head to your room, aware you haven't breathed in a couple of minutes.

Theatres are fantastical places, but they keep their secrets. The stage door is the drawbridge, and the stage manager is the keeper. To know them, and be allowed free passage by them, is never without a tingle down the spine.

Simon Evans

The Duchess Theatre

Before I was an actor stage doors were always mysterious to me. The only thing I knew about them was that they were where you went if you wanted to catch a glimpse of the actors you'd just watched in a show. I often wondered what was through those doors, and hoped that one day I'd find out. Jump forward a few years and I finally walk through those doors, greeted by the friendliest, warmest and perhaps most knowledgeable people in the building, and see what thousands of other people have seen before – the bit of the theatre that's hidden, this huge sprawling maze of corridors, offices, green room, rehearsal rooms, costume department, prop store and dressing rooms. The heart of the theatre, and all of it just beyond the stage door.

Fisayo Akinade

The joy of walking out of a stage door and seeing the faces of people who have just experienced your work can never be equalled. Especially when you meet familiar faces or faces that you've not seen in decades. Once I met a friend from school who I had not seen in 25 years. All of a sudden, you are meeting their husband, wife or children. A stage door is a magical place where some even meet their future partner.

The Prince Edward Theatre

From an early age the stage door was for me,
a portal into a different and secret world,
no matter how shabby its location, it was an
Exclusive Private Club, a sort of Temple into which only the chosen few were permitted to enter.
Once inside it seemed I was trespassing on
the experience I'd had in the auditorium and its magic.
I have that feeling still.
Even now, if I'm working in a particular theatre, going through that
Portal means I have to change.

Zoë Wanamaker

The Bridge Theatre

INDEX

ACKNOWLEDGEMENTS

First, thank you to all the individuals who contributed to this book, who took the time to muse over what stage doors mean to them.

Also, thank you to Will Dady, Max Moore, and Zeynep Kazmaz for their patience in helping us publish this book.

Special thanks to you, the reader. By buying this book you have contributed to the following charities that are supporting the theatre industry as it gets back on its feet:

The Actors' Benevolent Fund, ArtsMinds and Theatre Artists Fund.

For over 135 years, **The Actors' Benevolent Fund** has supported actors and stage managers experiencing hardship due to injury, illness or old age.

For more information, please visit www.actorsbenevolentfund.co.uk

Theatre Artists Fund has been created to provide emergency support for theatre workers and freelance professionals across the UK in need of urgent and critical financial support due to the devastating impact of Covid-19 on the theatre sector.

For more information, please visit www.theatreartists.fund

ArtsMinds is a collaborative initiative from BAPAM (British Association of Performing Arts Medicine), Equity, Spotlight and The Stage to bring together into one place a raft of resources for performers and creative practitioners facing mental health issues